In Manchester Square, June 1, 1975

MANCHESTER SQUARE

Edward Dorn & Jennifer Dunbar

PERMANENT PRESS
LONDON & NEW YORK
1975

ISBN 0 905258 00 2

For Robert & Tatiana

HOME AGAIN

I bought a key to the square
for two guineas, that denomination
a remoter clue than it once was.
And we can't take Tassie
although it is said
she crawls under the gate.

Nicholas invariably goes to Selfridges
to confer with the manager of model airplanes.
Kid likes the colour TV
and Maya's Gladys comes to straighten the flat.

Growing on the rooftop garden
the plants of the gays across the street
have grown younger
the avocados in the Mansions are stronger.
The gulls are circling the chimney pots
wheeling around the spires of Marylebone
dining at precisely four every afternoon
on the roof of the Coachmakers Arms.
Seeds of wind blow down in the rain
upon the plane of a dreamy day
watering the sensations of Holmes and Freud.

MANCHESTER SQUARE

Autumn

Leaves falling all over the square
turning the grass and flower beds
into a Monet air when the sun comes out
everything glows with the oily richness

Winter

The mist is blowing thru the plane trees
under the taxis, around the children playing
past the gates of the Wallace Collection
to the chair I pulled out of the shadows
into the sun and it fills my lungs
to return as song with the winter roses

Spring

Long brown shadows
slanting across the green grass
on an evening staged in London orange
rings of daffodils are dancing
around the boles of the plane trees

BOND STREET STASH

Out of the full sun
chords of an accordian
breathing Sorrento
from the warm tubes
over the fanatic mind
all the way down
the rushing back stairs
all the way down
the brain so pleased
to be in a spiral
descending to the trains
on its very own legs.

GROSVENOR SQUARE

Several registers down from charming
several temperatures lower than elsewhere.

There are some amusements on the east side:
the very ordinary chevy limousines
in front of the Canadian Embassy
and next door, at the French Embassy
always breathing,
one lone over-bred Daimler
weak in the front quarters
a strong, rather literal trunk.

Over on the west side the bronze eagle
unaccountably without a perch
grossly attractive, one *could* say
Profound Bad Taste, and it has been said
but here again we are confronted by failure.
Just visible thru the trees
a ribbon streaming from its beak.

MOUNT STREET

This ninety-five pound hound
squatting by the kerb
has turned much food to sauce
under the glove and smile of his boss.

The residual now deposited on the street
is his masters answer to the roman conference
now complete.

Even now, some well lasted heel
in motion from an unknown origin
marches toward mañana
and in the first moment of disgust
will mistake this thing for a banana.

AUDLEY

Antique shotguns by appointment
cut glass & porcelain elephants
enameled & brass backways
fretted by the ghosts of tradesmen
clamoring for the days of epicurism & lust.

And out front in the wind
a parade of self-conscious coats
which are going to look very odd
when they get back home, vanha kaveri?

ST. CHRISTOPHER'S PLACE

It was raining, it was afternoon
it was dark, it was one of those days.
A woman was dying on the cobblestones.
Thru the small crowd of shoppers
and shopkeepers, French from the antique market
Japanese from the restaurants
real London people from the smart boutiques
I could see the Swiss shop
where I bought a velvet jacket in November.

They made a bed out of their coats
and a canopy out of their bright umbrellas
for her raft of death in the pedestrian river.
Under the wheeling gulls
looking for the scraps of lunch
a crew sets up to shoot an ad
the giant lights look sternly down
as a professional model
steps from the cafe
holding the beginning of a smile in her hand.

CARLOS PLACE

Dangerous crossing.

The deeper mysteries of the body
repose in fur, and the human face
is ritualized in paint
but not broadly
as in the faces of Melanesia.

Two men, from the backside
walk briskly in step, definitely
hanging in their pants, American
officialdom ought to do something
about their costumes,
if they would learn the art
of inconspicuousness.

They are not hit men
but they might know hit men
and when Kid runs ahead
to St. Georges, I have a nervousness
alternating between the rude traffic
and the potential
but perhaps only reputational crossfire.
It is all implied thru international contracts.
London, after all, is a busy and important city.

And by extrapolation there is this smallest
viral emanation on the porch of the Connaught,
one of our periodic haunts.

The Retainers, shuffling their gung ho
with their gung fu, then, bored with that
they throw their eyes like dice
across the grey felt of a tabloid.
Rape, pillage, famine, Lord Lucan, cannibalism,
plus a breathless reduction of the boring essentials,
a yawn into Portuguese events
a scratch on the hind leg for Lon Nol
that winters major palindrome remember
one blink for Wallace, a gesture to the perverse,
shaking hands out of a wheel chair
a cold fleeting glance at Sihanouks chauffeur.

The real people here
are expensive old ladies, who
stare like Egyptians out of stone
behind their masks of weathered experience
their service done, and they know
how they have lasted. They wait for the Big cars.

Carlos Place is the one stretch
you can't avoid, it's the transit line
between the squares
at one end is the valve of money
at the other end the valve of policy.

BACKSTREET SOCIETY

On the way back from school
we are on schedule for the teabreak
at Weighhouse and Binney Street.
The cafe swarms with taxidrivers.

This is our favorite street:
even the Revlon lipstick fatory is serious.

Every morning, in a smart little cottage
at Dukes yard, a Mercedes is parked
its pistons mumbling
and the chauffeur hissing like a Ukranian
thru a cracked door at the meter-maid
always dutifully and impartially
writing out a ticket.

It is no wonder they can't come to an agreement
the difference between communist and socialist habit
is not subtle.

DEAR HERBIE

I left my room key
in the pigeon hole
there are some books there
I forgot to mention
please take them, even
if they scream out
that they are not
worthy of your attention.

MANCHESTER SQUARE

Our friends portray the time here.
Last week, when the sun swung low
I held the notebook and wrote
a letter in the breeze
just at the beginning of winter.

The dim traffic of Oxford Street
silhouetted in the sun
thru the Wigmore veil
knotted with the original guards
of international business machines.

A few new pieces inlay the decade,
like the all-night tobacconist
and some blown away,
like the eyes of Selfridges.

The growth is still careful here.
The plane trees are an expression
of their upkeep
while the flow that threatens them bends
an apparent and profuse
dissension of the tongue.

But the green hand still
gently rocks the cradle.
This garden is going to be
difficult to destroy.

600 copies of this first edition, of which 100 are specially bound in heavy wrappers and are numbered and signed by the authors, were published in December 1975 as number six in the Permanent Press series by Robert Vas Dias, 52 Cascade Avenue, London, N.10. England, and 1040 Park Avenue, New York, New York 10028, U.S.A.